W9-CDW-559

Everything You Need to Know About

LIVING IN A FOSTER HOME

More teens are living in foster homes than ever before.

Everything You Need to Know About

LIVING IN A FOSTER HOME

Joseph Falke

THE ROSEN PUBLISHING GROUP, INC.
NEW YORK

I would like to thank the following people for their assistance:

All the foster teens who shared their times of trial and success with me. Mr. and Mrs. Gonzales, Mr. and Mrs. Penwick, and Mr. and Mrs. Tauch.

The Texas Department of Protective and Regulatory Services, particularly Mary Miller, MSW, CSW; Delma Ochoa, Protective Service Specialist; Bill Whipple, Information Specialist.

Medina Children's Home, Medina, Texas, particularly Kenneth Wilson, CCAL, BA, LSW, MS.

Boys' Ville of Converse, Texas, particularly Mrs. Lenna Baxter and Mrs. Melody Jay.

Published in 1995 by The Rosen Publishing Group, Inc.
29 East 21st Street, New York, NY 10010

Copyright 1995 by The Rosen Publishing Group, Inc.

in the United States of America

ibrary of Congress Cataloging-in-Publication Data

Everything you need to know about living in a foster home / Joe Falke. — 1st ed.
    p.   cm. — (The Need to know library)
Includes bibliographical references and index.
Summary: Gives examples of teenagers who have been sent to live with foster families, detailing some of the reasons for needing foster care, what to expect, and how to make the necessary adjustments.
    ISBN 0-8239-1873-4
    1. Foster home care—United States—Juvenile literature.
2. Foster children—United States—Juvenile literature.   3. Foster parents—United States—Juvenile literature.   [1. Foster home care.]   I. Title.   II. Series.
HV881.F35   1995
362.7'33'0973—dc20
                                                            94-44968
                                                               CIP
                                                               AC

Contents

Introduction

Many of today's teens are faced with parents who are abusive, addicted to drugs or alcohol, or do not know how to handle their emotions, especially anger. The result is that more teens are in foster care than ever before. Whatever the reason for foster care, it is important to know that the teen is not at fault for leaving home.

Foster care is not something new, and it is not something negative. The first foster teen in America was Benjamin Eaton in the early 1700s. That means that foster care has been around for nearly three hundred years, which has given us a little time to practice. The author of this book was in foster care for more than twelve years.

All foster teens share one thing: They have a parent with a problem and must live away from the parent. So remember that you are not alone.

This book is about foster teens who have both short and long stays in new homes. It looks at what kinds of homes there are. It looks at foster parents and their roles. It looks at the feelings and problems you may have in foster care and ways to a solution. It discusses what to expect and how to deal with your return to your family. It discusses your rights and responsibilities as a foster teen and the opportunities for your future.

This book also talks about something very important: understanding that being a foster teen does not make you a less important person, and that people do care about you.

The birth parents of foster children are usually either unwilling or unable to care for their children properly.

Chapter 1

Who Is a Foster Child?

A parent may have a problem that disrupts the life of a family. The other members of that family may have to seek an alternative home to receive the nurturing and structured conditions needed to become successful, productive, and happy.

Teenagers are at a time in life that is critical to their development. They are searching for an adult identity. If their parent is unable to care for them, that does not mean others cannot or will not.

For example, if two brothers do not get along, they don't necessarily hate or even dislike each other. Nor does it prevent them from having other friends if they prefer not to be together.

This is the root of foster care. It is the parenting version of seeking friends in time of need.

Neglect

*Maria's mother was addicted to drugs. Maria
had cared for her mother and her brother Jose for as
long as she could remember. Then Jose was badly
hurt in a fall. Someone had to sign for his surgery
at the hospital, but at 15 Maria wasn't old enough.
She told the authorities at the hospital where she
lived and explained why her mother was not
present.*

*The police called Social Protective Services, a
state agency that cares for neglected, abused, or
abandoned young people. The agency finds homes
for teenagers and provides clothing and medical
care when a parent is unwilling or unable to do
so.*

*Social Protective Services sent a caseworker to
meet with Maria. A caseworker is a person who
finds foster parents for a teenager and makes sure
the teen is cared for. Maria was a little suspicious of
entering a new situation, because she had taken
care of her brother and herself for so long.*

*The caseworker introduced Maria to Mr. and
Mrs. Garcia, who were foster parents. The Garcias
had two children of their own, a daughter of 17 and
a son of Maria's age.*

*"At first I didn't understand why these people were
telling me that I couldn't take care of my family,"
says Maria. "I was pretty angry. I also felt guilty, as
if I had turned my mother in. I cried all the time,
and I threw things. I guess I was hoping that if I*

Some teens try to care for siblings when parents don't.

No one has the right to abuse you.

broke enough things they might let me go. But breaking things only made me feel worse.

"After some counseling, I began to realize that I was really angry at my mother because she had chosen drugs over us.

"Jose still has a long way to go. He is always in trouble. He still blames his caseworker and foster parents for everything."

Maria's mother died of a drug overdose two years after Maria and her brother went into foster care. Maria is now eighteen and is studying to be a nurse.

"I can't believe this is happening to me!" she says. "I used to do so poorly in school. My foster sister, Delma, helped me with my hard subjects, and I started to feel good about learning. It's great to work at something and succeed!"

Abuse

Sheila's father was an alcoholic. She had experienced many days when her father lost his temper and beat her in his anger. Sometimes the beatings were so bad that they left cuts and bruises. Whenever her friends asked about them, Sheila said she was clumsy.

One day a teacher noticed a swelling on Sheila's face and sent her to the nurse. Sheila had not told anyone that her father hit her, but the nurse guessed that something was not right. She called Protective Services.

After having a talk with Sheila's father, the

caseworker, Mr. Darnell, decided that she should not go home. Sheila was relieved that she had not had to tell on her father, but that something was being done to protect her from further beatings. Her father was quick to anger, and she was afraid. Mr. Darnell asked for an emergency placement, which is done when it is dangerous for a teen to remain at home.

Mr. Darnell began the search for a foster home for Sheila. The court had placed a restraining order on her father, and the police would be sure to keep him away. Under the restraining order, Sheila's father was forbidden to go near or even talk to her. If he did, he could go to jail. Sheila finally felt safe from her father.

The Unfit Parent

Jim's father was a traveling salesman. His mother had recently suffered a debilitating stroke. Jim, 15, didn't know how to deal with his mother's condition in the absence of his father. He began to look for ways to avoid being at home. His friends persuaded him to stay out all night when his father wasn't around. Most often they hung out down by the lake, drinking.

One night, Jim's friends decided to steal a car. Jim wasn't sure it was a good idea, but it was easier to go along than to fight it and be called chicken. They were caught about ten minutes into *the joyride. Jim's friends were sent to reform school, a prison for juveniles. Because of Jim's circumstances, the judge was a little more lenient with him.*

He ordered a home study for Jim and his parents. A caseworker examines a teen's home life to see if it is balanced enough to allow him to grow up in a healthy environment. After speaking with Jim's teachers, his parents, and other people related to the family, the caseworker told the judge what he had discovered.

The judge decided that Jim was not delinquent, but that he needed parental supervision. His father couldn't quit his job, and his mother could not care for him. The only option left for Jim was mandatory placement in a foster home for one year.

This home was a residential care facility, which is a campus with many houses. Each house has house parents and its own rules.

Abandonment

Mike was 13 when he first went to a foster home. His mother was an alcoholic, and his father had left them when Mike was a baby.

One of Mike's teachers called Protective Services because Mike often came to school without lunch or lunch money. On the first freezing day of winter, Mike came to school with

Teachers are required to report any signs of suspected child abuse that they observe in their students.

only a T-shirt, jeans, and a bad cold. The school also had reports of Mike's eating out of the cafeteria garbage cans after school.

Mike laughs as he recalls his situation. "I can't believe how bad it used to be. I didn't have many clothes. I can't remember eating a real meal, except when I was at a friend's house. I think people gave me strange looks at how I would eat almost everything in sight.

"My real mom . . . Well, she was always drunk. I don't know where she got the money to drink with.

"At first when my receiving caseworker, Mr. Ryan, took me in, I was pretty mad. I tried to run *away. I had grown up doing pretty much what I wanted.*

"It's funny to say this now, since I am almost eighteen and getting ready for college, but going to foster care was good for me. Almost all my friends from before have been in juvenile detention or are in a reformatory.

"I hate to think where I might be if my sixth-grade teacher hadn't called Protective Services. When I stopped being mad and pushing my foster father away, things got better. Back then, I didn't want to listen to anyone. I told my caseworker off, but she didn't get unglued. She took me to counseling and finally my foster dad would take me.

"I found out that I was actually angry with my real parents. I have to admit that I love my foster dad and mom, but I sure wanted to hate somebody when I first got here."

Mike also says that he enjoys having a foster mom who cooks real meals and a foster dad who scuba dives with him at a local lake. Mike is proud that he earned money for his own scuba gear. He works at a fast-food restaurant near his neighborhood.

"My foster parents had to get on to me about school a lot, but they helped me when they could," *Mike recalls. "I still feel bad about how I treated them at first. Now I'm looking forward to college and studying marine biology. If there was one*

thing I'd tell a foster kid about his new home, it would be: 'Chill out and coast with the ride for a while. See where it really goes before you do anything rash.'"

Chapter 2

Going to a Foster Home

Usually foster teens are placed with families of their own ethnic background. Sometimes this is not possible when there is a shortage of foster homes.

Caseworkers know it is hard enough to be apart from a mother or father. They know it is much harder when a teen must adjust to different traditions, foods, and sometimes a different language. Caseworkers try hard to find the home best suited for a particular teen.

It is natural to be curious or concerned about your new foster family. You may have many questions and perhaps a few fears.

Will they like me?
Will it be very different from my home?
Will the people be strange? Will I be strange to them?

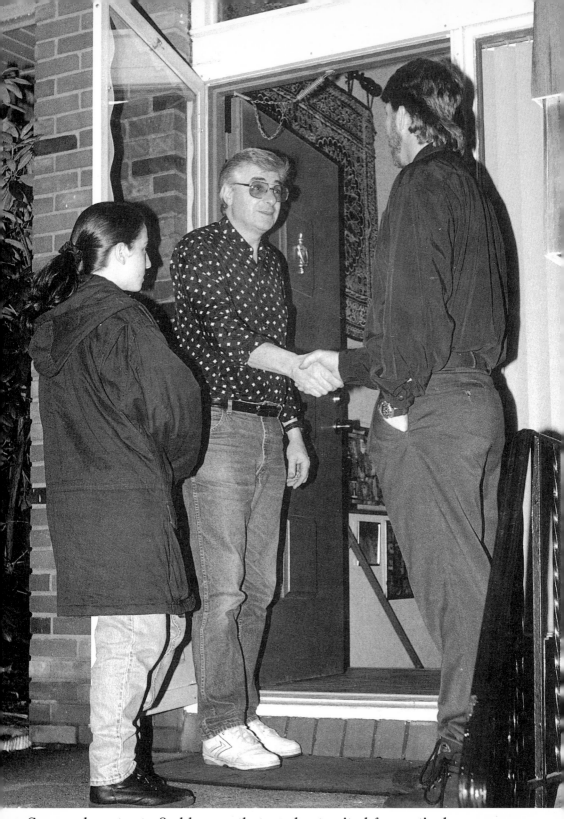

Caseworkers try to find homes that are best suited for particular teens.

What if my brother or sister cannot come with
me?

The best way to overcome your concerns is to
talk to your new family. Find out what they like to
do. What kind of television shows do they watch?
Do they go to church on Sundays? If it is summer,
do they like to go swimming? If it is winter, do
they like to ice skate? If you do not ice skate and
they do, are you willing to learn? Learning new
things to do is one way to become part of a new
family.

Families have rules that they expect their own
teenagers to follow. Most foster teens discover that
there are more rules and different ones in a foster
home. Those who are not accustomed to any rules
may find it difficult when they are held
accountable for their behavior.

Adjusting to a New Home

*Patrick's family had no rules. As long as no one
called to complain, his parents didn't care what
he did. Patrick ate whatever there was in the
house. He had no curfew. He had no extra clothes.
What little he had, he usually stole. When
Patrick's father was in town, the parents went out
drinking. They didn't care where he was, or what
he did, provided that he created no problems for
them.*

Late one night, Patrick and some of his friends robbed a convenience store and ran away. A car struck Patrick and broke his back. Patrick's mother was out on the town, and it was a couple of days before she finally came home.

After almost a year in the hospital, Patrick was placed in a foster home.

"The rules. That is the hardest part about a foster home," says Patrick. "Now I see things differently. All these rules are to help me. My bus comes last, so I have the bathroom last in the morning. It is hard for me to get around, so everyone else has to be up and dressed before me. My foster brother, Kareem, complained at first. The rules seem to center around me, and it made me very self-conscious, but I can see why we need them."

Kareem arrived at the foster home two years after Patrick. Both have now lived there for more than five years. Kareem too had trouble with the rules.

"Patrick is right," says Kareem. "The rules were a pain. When I came here, I couldn't get out the window at night. Patrick's bed was in front of the window so he was in the way. Deep inside, I was glad. I saw what sneaking out and running around had done to Patrick. I always thought I would die as part of a gang or something, because I had no real future. Part of me misses the freedom of being with my friends, but the other

One of the most difficult things to adjust to in a foster home can be the new rules.

part of me sees the light at the end of a very dark tunnel. I think now I really have something to look forward to.

"The strange part is that even my gang had rules. As wild and mean as we were, we still had rules. Now I'm the only one going anywhere. Two of my friends are dead from gang shootings. Another is in a coma at a hospital, and I think the rest are locked up in juvenile detention. A part of me wants to forget my past and another part wants to help stop the gangs."

Kareem begins college in a year to become a social worker. Patrick has developed an interest in electronics and has a Technician's class ham radio license. He plans to attend vocational training for computer repair.

Living in a structured environment has given new life to Patrick and Kareem. For people to get along, there must be rules for what is acceptable and not acceptable: a time to eat, a time for school, a time for chores, and a time for the fun things.

Having chores to do is part of belonging to a real family. Everyone must do their share: someone takes out the garbage, another does the dishes, another cleans house. One person cannot do it all.

Living Apart

Brothers and sisters can live together if the foster home can handle a large family. Sometimes brothers and sisters may have to live apart for a while, but even so, visiting is possible.

The state or city makes rules for foster homes. These rules include the minimum number of rooms in the home and the size of the rooms for each member of the family. Foster families are limited in the number of teens they may care for. If they have teenagers of their own, that reduces the number of foster teens they have in their home.

Breaking Up a Family

Cheryl, Daniel, Matt, and Shari are brothers

Chores are often part of your responsibilities in a foster home.

and sisters. Cheryl and Daniel are 15 and 14; Matt and Shari are 9 and 7. Unfortunately, no single foster family can take them all. Cheryl and Shari live with the Smith family, and Daniel and Matt live with the Mayhews.

"When Mom and Dad were killed, I couldn't deal with all of us brothers and sisters being split apart," says Cheryl. "Our caseworker introduced the Smiths and the Mayhews to each other when they met with us kids. We were an emergency placement, so we all met at the Protective Services building. It was a very bad time for all of us."

"The Smiths and the Mayhews were wonderful through the ordeal. Trina Smith, Jack and Nancy's daughter, gave up her room and moved in with her sister, Deenie. They took us to our parents' funerals, and they were very understanding.

"I guess my worst day was when I burned the toast at breakfast. I don't know why, but I started to cry and couldn't stop. No one overreacted to my problem. Nancy talked to me, and my caseworker arranged for counseling. I found out later that I was suffering from acute depression.

"The Smiths and the Mayhews arranged to visit each other. One Saturday the Mayhews would come over to the Smiths' home and we would have burgers and swim. The following Saturday we would drive out to the Mayhews' to barbecue and ride horses. The Smiths live in the city, and

the Mayhews live about 15 miles out in the country.

"Both families happen to go to the same church in the city, the Mayhews to the early service, and the Smiths to late service. They didn't know this until after the accident. Then we all started going to early service. After church, we would visit out in the parking lot for a while."

Cheryl laughed. "Sometimes we visited so long that second service would let out. Often, Jack Smith and Bill Mayhew would just go pick up fried chicken for twelve and we would have a picnic in the parking lot. Finally the church put two picnic tables under the big oak tree, just for us."

Residential Home

Todd's grandmother died two years ago. Since then, he has been placed in two foster homes. The first was a military family, who were transferred away. His second home was an elderly couple who decided it was time to stop caring for foster teens. Moving from family to family was taking an emotional toll on Todd.

Todd has no other relatives, but the foster family concept has become difficult for him to accept. He decided to ask his caseworker to allow him a transfer to a residential home. A residential home can care for many teens. Some are just for

Residential homes often house both boys and girls.

boys or just for girls, but most are for both boys and girls.

A residential care facility is a campus with many houses. Each house has a set of house parents and separate rules. Not all residential homes are alike. Some have dormitories. Some have counselors instead of house parents. The foster teens in residential home care are there for different reasons, just as in other foster homes.

The needs of the teens determine where they are placed. Regardless of the type of home, cooperation and understanding are the key ingredients for making a foster situation work.

Rules help people develop self-discipline to live

with each other and achieve goals. Both the foster parent and the foster teen have a responsibility to each other. The foster parent has agreed to help provide for and guide the foster teen through adolescence. The foster teen has the responsibility of allowing the foster parent to accomplish that goal.

When both people strive to meet their responsibilities, the foster teen has endless opportunities to achieve whatever he or she wants to accomplish in life.

Chapter 3

Foster Parents

Foster parents are people who like helping others. They are not paid very much for what they do. Money is not their reason for being foster parents. Some foster parents may not have children of their own.

Fred and Ina are a retired couple whose own kids are grown, but they enjoy being active parents. Many teenagers enjoy Fred and Ina's small farm.

It takes six months to a year to become a foster parent. A lot of training and special classes are involved. Not everyone is cut out to be a foster parent. Some of the requirements of foster parents are:

- Their age
- Their income and ability to handle money
- The number of children they have

It takes a lot of training to become foster parents.

- The size of their home, which must also must pass a fire, health, and safety inspection
- Suitable transportation, which may be a public bus or train
- Their health
- A clean background
- Letters of reference from both relatives and nonrelatives

If they meet all these requirements, they must take a special training course.

Some teens may have special problems. Foster parents are allowed to choose the type of problems they can handle. Even though requirements may be different from state to state, these are basically the

You can stay in contact with your natural parents even if you are living in a foster home.

expectations of a foster parent. A foster parent must think that you are very important to go through the difficulty of qualifying.

Mr. and Mrs. Mantz have provided foster care for more than twelve years.

"We have four grown children of our own and ten grandchildren. We love all of our kids, both foster and natural. Some of the teens who come to us have had a bad time, but we know that it comes from poor family habits. That's no excuse for continuing on a bad road in life. Don and I try to be patient and help them learn a better way. It's sad to see young adults who can't make sound decisions because they were never taught how. It brings me real happiness when one of my foster children comes back to see me and has done well.

"I wish I could tell all the foster kids that you can be as great as you want to be. You are special because of who you are. If you don't like something about yourself, work with your foster parent and caseworker to change it. Take the chance that is being offered to you."

You will probably discover that you like your foster parent. That is not bad. There is nothing wrong with it. You are not being disloyal to your real parents. If you feel guilty because you like your foster parents, talk to your caseworker. She or he can help you find a way to overcome this feeling.

A foster parent is not trying to replace a natural parent. Some parents may feel threatened by the foster parent's role, but foster parents want to do what is best for their foster teen. Mrs. Mantz had this problem with the mother of a foster son.

"Danny was nine when he came to us. He was one of our first foster boys and was with us for seven years. His own mother was not very reliable, and when Danny heard the other foster kids calling Don and me Mom and Dad, after a while he did also.

"When his mother came to visit, Danny referred to me as Mom. Danny's mother was an insecure person and became upset. She threatened Danny never to come to see him again. She was already on shaky ground: Her visits were haphazard— sometimes at bad times of the day and occasionally at night.

"She didn't care how much she upset Danny as long as she had her way. Danny was torn over what to do, and I told him that he could do whatever he wanted. Good parents do not seek to torment their children.

"The problem was basically resolved with Danny calling Don and me what our grandchildren call us: Mo-mo and Po-po. Danny's mother eventually vanished, and he remained with us until he was 16 and went to a residential home. Danny still felt guilty even after he was

Foster parents often help to fill the gaps that birth parents left, such as teaching the teen to read.

older. Only now does he really realize that his mother was making an excuse to leave him."

Danny is now an underwater welder for an offshore oil company. He is married and still visits his foster parents often.

Mentoring

When foster parents take on the responsibility of caring for a foster teen, they know that the natural parents have had difficulty providing care. It is their only desire to help a foster teen find the road to success.

Mr. Washington is a civilian electronics

supervisor at a local military base. He is responsible for adjusting or repairing communication and navigational systems of military transports. He and his wife are the foster parents of Robert, who is crippled for life.

"When Robert first came here, he was bent on self-destruction. Having no hope does that to a person. I knew that we needed to give him hope of carrying on a normal life, even from a wheelchair.

"I also knew that even if Robert could walk, if he had stayed in his original home, he would probably have dropped out of school. A dropout is three times more likely to be unemployed. The biggest problem for the unemployed is that they can't find a place in the workforce because they don't have an education.

"When Robert accepted being confined to a wheelchair, I began to work with him on his schoolwork. His biggest problem was that he did not like to read. First, I had him read short fun books. Then we moved on to longer books with more complex plots."

Mrs. Washington inserted a comment, "And now we can't get him to stop. He is constantly reading. If not reading, then playing with Harold's computer or sending code on his ham radio."

"That is true," Mr. Washington admitted. "He stays pretty busy for someone who has lost so much

mobility. One thing I think is important for teenagers to know is that I think everyone is smart. I believe intelligence is nothing more than confidence in your ability to learn. If you believe you can, you will. If you believe you can't, you won't. I did not say you won't have to work at developing your educational skills.

"It's like Robert's reading. The more he did, the better he became. The better he became, the more he liked it. He worked at bettering himself, and now he is one smart kid!"

There is no doubt that the Washingtons are very proud of Robert. With Mr. Washington's help, Robert completely designed and built his own shortwave radio. This is an excellent example of what can be accomplished when foster parents and foster teens pull together to accomplish a goal.

Not all foster parents are married. Janie is a single schoolteacher who cares for a foster teen, Angie. She and Angie are almost like sisters. Angie was fifteen when her mother vanished, and she has lived with Janie since then.

"Sometimes Angie forgets that I am the foster parent. Fortunately, I don't need to remind her too often. Angie calls me Janie, and I think that's okay. We are more like very close friends.

"I don't think our situation would work for everyone—especially those teenagers who won't

take no for an answer. But Angie is very mature for her age."

Angie's favorite pastime is ice skating. She started skating when she first came to live with Janie two and half years ago. Though an avid skater herself, Janie does not compete. She enjoys watching and working with Angie.

These are the some of the people who become foster parents. Remember that the foster teen and the foster parent make the team for achievement in our fast-paced world. There are many opportunities in the world, and many people willing to help you find them. Relax and enjoy the time you have with your foster family. You may discover it is the best of times!

Chapter 4

Coping

If you feel that your life is going from bad to worse, you are not alone. Teenage years are difficult enough and are probably more so when you are in a foster home. Adolescence is a time when your body is changing rapidly. Your senses are telling you conflicting things, some youthful information and some adult information. That is why you need foster parents to help you deal with these changes.

Finding a Way to Cope

It is difficult to accept, but some of your decisions may not be in your best interest. Overcoming problems can be handled by making the right decisions. Some people cannot see an approaching problem or the best decision because they are on the inside looking out.

Most mature adults can see a problem coming up because they have seen it before, maybe in themselves or in a friend they grew up with. This is experience. For example, to know that a stove is really hot, some people touch it and get burned. Others observe the act and know not to do it. Some need only to be told.

This is what a pregnant teen, Terry, had to say of her lack of experience.

"My life seemed to be a disaster after 12 or 13. I couldn't talk to my parents. They didn't understand me.

"I met Jake when I was 15 and he was 17. He understood everything I was going through. I trusted Jake and I didn't trust my parents.

"I realize now that Jake knew only a little more than I knew. His lack of experience coupled with his immaturity left me in a difficult situation."

Terry suffered much from believing in the experience of a person not much older than herself. This is where having good parents comes in. Having foster parents may make it harder for you to trust, since you may already feel betrayed by a parent.

You need the guidance of experience as you experiment with stepping out into the world. That is why rules and boundaries are established. Experience usually comes with time, and with time

Friends can be great sources of influence, both positive and negative.

comes age. That is why people who are older have charge of those who are younger.

Peer Groups

Teens tend to be very critical of themselves. They look to their peers to judge how they look, how they sound, and how they act. When life is difficult, teens seek out friends who share their difficulties. If these friends handle their difficulties badly, the teen may suffer the same fate.

Reaching for an identity in a group is good, but it needs to be a positive identity. Reaching out to a peer group that is not positive can have disastrous results.

Rick's mother and stepfather were having marital difficulties. Problems had developed, and Rick lost the ability to confide in either of them. He began spending more time with his cousin John's group, who were not the best of role models. John sold drugs and guns to gangs.

"I thought John knew everybody and everything." Rick says. "At seventeen, he seemed to have his life together. On the other hand, my mom and stepfather never seemed to even act their age. Mom worked in a bar and never came home after work. My stepfather began acting single, so after a while no one came home anymore.

"John was older and had a car. After hanging around with him I stopped going to school. I came and went as I pleased. I was one step ahead of the truant officer, and I didn't care. John had quit school two years earlier, and he looked like he had it made. If I was sixteen, I would have quit school too.

"Then one day it happened: John left me holding a gun when a bust went down. We had stopped at his house to get some guns John had to sell. He couldn't carry them all, so he handed me one. It was a .38 caliber. Outside at a car, John sold all the guns and asked me for the last one. Suddenly cops were everywhere. We took off. I went one way and John went the other. I heard two shots, and later found out that John had fired

at the cops while they chased him. The police couldn't find John, but they found me.

"I told the truth to the police. They tried to find my mom and my stepfather, but it took three days. It didn't take much to convince the judge that I was fending for myself. The judge arranged for me to live in a residential home instead of sending me to a reformatory."

Running Away

In a bad situation, running away sounds like a great idea. But when you leave a place, it's more than likely that you'll take the problem with you.

If you choose to stay and work out the problem, you choose to invest in yourself. When you work it out, you are better off than if you had tried to run from it.

Jeremy was three when he first came to foster care. His mom would keep him for a while and then drop him off at a shelter when she couldn't care for him. The authorities would place Jeremy in foster care. After a time, his mother would take him out of the state.

When Jeremy was 12, his mother was informed that if she removed Jeremy once more she would be charged with kidnapping. Jeremy has not seen his mother since, but she left behind a special problem for Jeremy, who is now 16.

"It is really hard when someone rejects you,"

Running away usually makes problems worse rather than better.

Jeremy says. "Whenever I thought someone was pushing me away or someone would punish me, or didn't like something about me, I thought it was rejection.

"If I even thought they were going to reject me, I might try to get ahead of the pain by running away. I didn't even understand it myself until I went to counseling. After I understood what to look for, I could take a stand and beat it. Then I began to develop real relationships."

Trust

Teens who have been in foster care are often highly sensitive to teasing and critical comments. They are also very critical of themselves and easily hurt. They often will not talk to friends about problems for fear of hearing criticism that they take as a form of rejection.

When foster teens see the closeness and support of a foster family, they may feel left out since it is not their family. Because of past rejections, they may not trust enough to reach out for the support being offered to them, fearing it may not be real.

Trusting Your Foster Parent

Telling someone about a problem is very hard. Whom shall I tell? Will they think I am silly? Will

honest and say what is really bothering you.

Anger

A person may be angry because of failing to understand why something is happening. Being mad for a long time can hurt a person inside or make him think things that are not true. Anger is not a bad thing, but what a person does with anger can be bad.

What is good in anger? Anger can make a person solve a problem, rather than do nothing about it. Anger is an emotion that arises when a person does not like or understand something. This can also cause frustration.

When you are angry or frustrated, you should first calm down. This can be done by breathing deeply and thinking of something else. After you are calm, you need to figure out the worst thing that can come from the problem that is making you angry. Accept it, even though you may not be able to change it right now.

Then go talk to the person involved in the problem. Remember, you need to take time in talking about the problem. You need to avoid acting in anger.

Depression

When Todd's grandmother died, he couldn't seem to stop crying. He had lost his parents when

Depression is a natural part of the grieving process.

he was young, and now his grandmother was gone. It was the worst pain he had ever felt. It was hard for him to believe it had happened.

Todd was *depressed* about his grandmother's death. Depression is feeling very bad about something for a long time.

After losing your parents you may even feel guilty about their deaths. Todd's grandmother had died while Todd was sleeping. He felt that if he had awakened earlier he might have been able to help her. That is not true. People cannot control when someone dies.

At times you cannot control your feelings. Todd was afraid that other boys would laugh at him for crying. Even though Todd was sixteen, it was okay for him to cry. Crying is part of mourning. Mourning is feeling sad about someone's death. It helps those who loved someone to release their feelings about that person. There is no right way or wrong way to mourn. Some people cry. Some people are quiet.

It would be impossible to cover every problem a person faces in foster care. If a problem is too difficult to talk to your foster parents about, talk to your caseworker. Ask how he or she would deal with it. You may need to talk to a counselor, a trained person who helps others with problems like anger, shame, guilt, or depression. There is nothing wrong about seeking help.

Chapter 5

Preparing for the Future

You may have asked yourself: Is there a future for me? The answer is: Your future is what you do today. What you choose to do each day determines where you will go tomorrow. Setting goals for tomorrow and making good decisions today help any dream come true.

Today is the first day of the rest of your life! There are many things to do in this world and many things to see. You may dream of climbing mountains, swimming the depths, soaring in the sky, or reaching for the stars. Dreams can come true, and here is how.

First we must understand why dreams don't come true.

Mistakes

People can make two kinds of mistakes. One

kind has a short-term effect and the other, a long-term effect.

An example of a short-term effect is failing a class if you decide not to study. A long-term effect is finding that you cannot get a good job after dropping out of school.

Making the right decisions is important. Relying on the right people is important too. Getting information from a friend who means well is a nice thought, but not very wise. This friend is probably your age and knows only as much as his or her life has allowed him or her to experience.

Would you ask your friend how to invest your money? Of course not! It is best to trust people who have experience.

Careers

Even big companies with many employees look outside the company to get the right answers. Finding the person who has the knowledge and experience is important before making a decision.

Going to see a career counselor is a good idea. Your school guidance counselor may be able to advise you about careers.

Some states offer free tuition, room, and board at state universities for foster children. Some community colleges have the same offer and make no charge at all for vocational training.

Welding, electronic and computer repair, or airframe and powerplant mechanic are some types of vocational training offered by community colleges. Even some types of nursing careers, like licensed vocational nurse, are offered. Many scholarships are available, especially for foster children.

Residential homes for children have counselors on staff. If you live in a foster home, your case-worker may be able to arrange for you to speak with a mentor, a person who can help you get where you want to go.

If you want to be a pilot, your mentor could help you find a pilot to talk with. If you want to be a businessman, he could introduce you to a local businessman. It is important to talk with people who do the jobs you may want to do.

When you are old enough, try to get a part-time job close to the field you are interested in. This is good experience, and you can save a little money for the unexpected. But remember, a job should never take the place of an education.

No one is born smart. Being smart is nothing more than believing in your ability to learn. If you open a book and tell yourself you cannot read it, you probably will not. If you open the book and say, "I am going to read this!" you probably will!

If you get used to doing things for yourself, everything else becomes easier. Learn to do for yourself. Accept help when you need it, but do whatever you can for yourself.

Succeeding means never giving up.

Quitters Never Win and Winners Never Quit

Someone asked a friend, "How is it you never fail at anything?"

The friend answered. "Oh, I fail. I just keep at it until I have it right. Then I go on to the next thing and keep at it until I get that right. I do it so much, I don't fail much anymore."

Life is not win or lose. It's keeping at something until you succeed. You may not succeed the first

time, but don't quit. Everyone makes mistakes and
has setbacks. Your setbacks may just look bigger
because they are *your* setbacks. Don't let *you*
discourage *yourself.*

Ask for help! That is why you have teachers,
foster parents, and caseworkers. If you ask an
honest question, you receive an honest answer. If
they don't know the answer, find someone who
does. But you must ask first.

Never make excuses for yourself. Accepting
responsibility is part of not making the same
mistake again. Pretending a failure is not your
fault when it is may cause you to make the same
mistake again.

No matter who you are, as long as you really try
and you seek help for your special problems, you
will succeed. But you must want to succeed. No
one can do it for you.

Also remember, there are many people who care
about you and want you to succeed and be happy.
Your caseworker is one of them. When you have
a problem and are uncomfortable talking with
others about it, your caseworker wants to help
you. But you must take the first step. No one
can read your mind. There is no such thing as a
stupid question except the one that goes unasked.

Self-Esteem

What is self-esteem? To esteem is to place value

on something. Self-esteem is self-value. It is important to believe in yourself. Everybody has problems or imperfections. It is important not to let a little problem look too big. Even big problems are usually made up of a few small problems.

Jerry thought he was a klutz. Jerry's real problem was that he was overweight and lacked coordination. How could he fix his problem? Jerry spoke to his coach at school. The coach told him to begin by fixing what he could fix the fastest: his coordination. He began tossing a ball with a friend. This built up his eye-hand coordination and was good exercise.

Jerry also worked on his weight. He loves to eat, so he began keeping track of the amount of fat he consumed every day. He knew that teenagers should eat less than 60 grams of fat per day. So Jerry ate very little fat, but lots of high-fiber foods. Then he did situps and pushups while he watched TV. Jerry lost the weight and felt better about himself.

By dealing with the little problems, Jerry solved the one big problem. Now he is headed to college with a sports scholarship and wants to be a professional baseball player.

As you can see, you are what you think you are. If a little voice inside you says, "I am an idiot" or "I can't do this," you will begin to believe it. You need to change the little voice.

When the little voice tells you something negative, stop and say, "I can do this!" "I am smart enough."

If you get a C on a test and you expected an A, you may be pushing yourself to failure. If you want the A, review why you got the C and work from there. Look for your stumbling blocks.

I became a foster child when I was five. I lived in three foster homes and then two residential care facilities. This was permanent placement until I was 18.

I didn't like school, and I didn't like to read. I knew that I needed to go to college one day, so I began to practice with small books. I practiced so much that now I like to read every night.

If someone had told me when I was young that one day I would be a Marine Corps fighter pilot and an author, I would not have believed it.

All the stories in this book are true. The names have been changed, but the people are real. All the people, including myself, were or are foster teenagers. The foster parents are real too.

As you can tell, attitude, cooperation, and perseverance have made most of us successful with our lives. Because you are one of us as a foster brother or sister, we care about you and want you to be successful too.

Glossary—*Explaining New Words*

abusive   Harmful or hurting another person.

alcoholic   Person addicted to alcohol.

adolescence   The period between 11 and 21, when one makes the transition to adulthood.

caseworker   A person who helps with problems.

child abuse   The deliberate harming of a child by an adult.

conflict   A problem or dispute between people.

cooperation   Working with another toward a common goal.

cope   To deal with problems or difficulties.

crisis   Emergency problem.

custody   Responsibility for the care or safety of others.

depression   Sadness, feeling of hopelessness.

emotional   Having to do with deep feelings.

frustration   Feelings of failure.

foster home   A home where teenagers may live when parents are unable to care for them.

foster parents   People who provide role models and care for teens in temporary homes.

mentor   Tutor, coach, or trusted guide.

neglect   Failure to care for a child.

residential care facility   A home environment consisting of houses or cottages, usually in a campus setting.

restraining order   Court order for the protection of an abused or harassed person.

Social Protective Services   Agency that specializes in providing assistance for teenagers with special family problems.

structured environment   Home or facility that provides conditions beneficial to teenagers.

Where to Go for Help

There are many special groups that can help you. Reach out to someone when you are having problems. People really want to help. These are some groups that can help with special needs.

Alcoholics Anonymous World Services
P.O. Box 459, Grand Central Station
468 Park Avenue South
New York, NY 10163

Child Welfare League of America (CWLA)
67 Irving Place
New York, NY 10003

Children's Bureau Clearinghouse on Child Abuse
    and Neglect Information
Department of Health and Human Services
P.O. Box 1182

Washington, DC 20013

Children's Defense Fund
1520 Madison Avenue NW
Washington, DC 20036

Drug and Alcohol Council
396 Alexander Street
Rochester, NY 14607

Families Anonymous
P.O. Box 528
14617 Victory Boulevard
Van Nuys, CA 91408

National Association of State Mental Health
    Societies
1001 Third Street SW
Washington, DC 20024

National Foster Parents Association (NFPA)
P.O. Box 16523
Clayton, MO 63105

Organization of Foster Families for Equality and
    Reform
P.O. Box 110
East Meadow, NY 11554

For Further Reading

Bauer, Marion Dane. *Foster Child*. New York: Seabury Press, 1977.

Blomquist, Geraldine Molettiere, and Blomquist, Paul. *Coping as a Foster Child*. New York: Rosen Publishing Group, 1991.

Byars, Betsy Cromer. *The Pinballs*. New York: Harper & Row, 1977.

Falke, Joseph. *Taking Wing*. New York: Random House, 1995.

Hall, Lynn. *Mrs. Portree's Pony*. New York: Scribner's, 1986.

MacLachlan, Patricia. *Mama One, Mama Two*. New York: Harper & Row, 1982.

Marker, Sherry. *Cooperation*. New York: Rosen Publishing Group, 1991.

McFarland, Rhoda. *Coping Through Self-Esteem*, rev. ed. New York: Rosen Publishing Group, 1993.

Index

About the Author

Joseph Falke lived in foster care for thirteen years, both in single-family environments and residential care facilities.

Mr. Falke is a retired Marine Corps fighter pilot. Now a free-lance writer for young people, he is the author of *Against the Odds* and *Taking Wing*, the latter of which is also currently being made into a film.

Mr. Falke is married and has one child. He remains very in-volved with his brothers and sisters of the Medina Children's Home.

Photo Credits

Cover, p. 28 by Lauren Piperno; pp. 2, 11, 20, 23, 31, 32, 35 by Kim Sonsky; p. 8 by Yung-Hee Chia; pp. 12, 25 by Marcus Schaffer; pp. 41, 44, 47, 49, 54 by Michael Brandt; p. 16 by Katherine Hsu.